Wolfgang Amadeus Mozart

SYMPHONIES NOS. 22–34

in Full Score

Wolfgang Amadeus Mozart

SYMPHONIES NOS. 22–34

in Full Score

From the
Breitkopf & Härtel Complete Works Edition

DOVER PUBLICATIONS, INC., NEW YORK

Published in Canada by General Publishing Company, Ltd., 30 Lesmill Road, Don Mills, Toronto, Ontario.
Published in the United Kingdom by Constable and Company, Ltd., 3 The Lanchesters, 162–164 Fulham Palace Road, London W6 9ER.

This Dover edition, first published in 1991, is an unabridged republication of Volume 2 of Series 8: *Symphonien* from *Wolfgang Amadeus Mozart's Werke. Kritisch durchgesehene Gesammtausgabe,* originally published by Breitkopf & Härtel, Leipzig, in 1880. Lists of instruments have been added.

Manufactured in the United States of America
Dover Publications, Inc., 31 East 2nd Street, Mineola, N.Y. 11501

Library of Congress Cataloging-in-Publication Data

Mozart, Wolfgang Amadeus, 1756–1791.
  [Symphonies. Selections]
  Symphonies nos. 22–34 / Wolfgang Amadeus Mozart.—In full score. 1 score.
  Reprint. Originally published: Leipzig : Breitkopf & Härtel, 1880 (Wolfgang Amadeus Mozart's Werke. Series 8, Symphonien ; v. 2).
  ISBN 0-486-26675-3 (pbk.)
  1. Symphonies—Scores.
  M1001.M92B69   1991
                                    90-754722
                                         CIP
                                          M

CONTENTS

INSTRUMENTATION

Symphony No. 22

2 Oboes [Oboi]
2 Horns (C) [Corni in C]
2 Trumpets (C) [Trombe in C]
Strings

Symphony No. 23

2 Oboes
2 Horns
2 Trumpets (D)
Strings

Symphony No. 24

2 Flutes [Flauti]
2 Oboes
2 Horns (B♭,E♭) [B,Es]
Strings

Symphony No. 25

2 Oboes
2 Bassoons [Fagotti]
4 Horns (B♭,G,E♭)
Strings

Symphony No. 26

2 Flutes
2 Oboes
2 Bassoons
2 Horns (E♭)
2 Trumpets (E♭)
Strings

Symphony No. 27

2 Flutes
2 Horns (G,D)
Strings

Symphony No. 28

2 Oboes
2 Horns (C,F)
2 Trumpets (C)
Strings

Symphony No. 29

2 Oboes
2 Horns (A,D)
Strings

Symphony No. 30

2 Oboes
2 Horns (D)
2 Trumpets (D)
Strings

Symphony No. 31

2 Flutes
2 Oboes
2 Clarinets (A) [Clarinetti in A]
2 Bassoons
2 Horns (D,G)
2 Trumpets (D)
Timpani
Strings

Symphony No. 32

2 Flutes
2 Oboes
2 Bassoons
4 Horns (G,D)
2 Trumpets (C)
Timpani
Strings

Symphony No. 33

2 Oboes
2 Bassoons
2 Horns (B♭ alto,E♭)
Strings

Symphony No. 34

2 Oboes
2 Bassoons
2 Horns (C)
2 Trumpets (C)
Timpani
Strings

SYMPHONY NO. 22
in C Major

K.162

Andantino grazioso.

Oboi.

Corni in C.

Violino I.

Violino II.

Viola I.

Viola II.

Violoncello e Basso.

SYMPHONY NO. 23
in D Major

K.181/162b

Andantino grazioso.

Presto assai.

SYMPHONY NO. 24
in B-flat Major

K.182/173dA

Allegro.

Oboi.

Corni in B.

Violino I.

Violino II.

Viola.

Violoncello e
Basso.

SYMPHONY NO. 25
in G Minor

K.183/173dB

Coda.

MENUETTO.

Oboi.

Corni in B.

Corni in G.

Violino I.

Violino II.

Viola.

Violoncello e Basso.

Oboe I.

Oboe II.

Fagotti.

Corni in G.

SYMPHONY NO. 26
in E-flat Major

K.184/161a

68   Symphony No. 26 in E-flat Major

72   Symphony No. 26 in E-flat Major

SYMPHONY NO. 27
in G Major

K.199/161b

82   Symphony No. 27 in G Major

SYMPHONY NO. 28
in C Major

K.200/189k

Menuetto D.C.

Coda.

SYMPHONY NO. 29
in A Major

K.201/186a

Coda.

Menuetto da capo

Allegro con spirito.

SYMPHONY NO. 30
in D Major

K.202/186b

MENUETTO.

Oboi.

Corni in D.

Trombe in D.

Violino I.

Violino II.

Viola.

Violoncello e
Basso.

Menuetto D.C.

Symphony No. 30 in D Major   153

154   Symphony No. 30 in D Major

SYMPHONY NO. 31
in D Major

K.297/300a

186   Symphony No. 31 in D Major

SYMPHONY NO. 32
in G Major

K.318

200   Symphony No. 32 in G Major

Andante.

210   Symphony No. 32 in G Major

211

SYMPHONY NO. 33
in B-flat Major

K.319

216   Symphony No. 33 in B-flat Major

Men. D. C.

Finale.
Allegro assai.

Oboi.

Fagotti.

Corni in B.

Violino I.

Violino II.

Viola.

Violoncello e
Basso.

SYMPHONY NO. 34
in C Major

K.338

I.

FINALE.

Allegro vivace.

Dover Orchestral Scores

THE SIX BRANDENBURG CONCERTOS AND THE FOUR ORCHESTRAL SUITES IN FULL SCORE, Johann Sebastian Bach. Complete standard Bach-Gesellschaft editions in large, clear format. Study score. 273pp. 9 × 12.   23376-6 Pa. **$10.95**

COMPLETE CONCERTI FOR SOLO KEYBOARD AND ORCHESTRA IN FULL SCORE, Johann Sebastian Bach. Bach's seven complete concerti for solo keyboard and orchestra in full score from the authoritative Bach-Gesellschaft edition. 206pp. 9 × 12.   24929-8 Pa. **$10.95**

THE THREE VIOLIN CONCERTI IN FULL SCORE, Johann Sebastian Bach. Concerto in A Minor, BWV 1041; Concerto in E Major, BWV 1042; and Concerto for Two Violins in D Minor, BWV 1043. Bach-Gesellschaft edition. 64pp. 9⅜ × 12¼.   25124-1 Pa. **$5.95**

GREAT ORGAN CONCERTI, OPP. 4 & 7, IN FULL SCORE, George Frideric Handel. 12 organ concerti composed by great Baroque master are reproduced in full score from the *Deutsche Handelgesellschaft* edition. 138pp. 9⅜ × 12¼.   24462-8 Pa. **$8.95**

COMPLETE CONCERTI GROSSI IN FULL SCORE, George Frideric Handel. Monumental Opus 6 Concerti Grossi, Opus 3 and "Alexander's Feast" Concerti Grossi—19 in all—reproduced from most authoritative edition. 258pp. 9⅜ × 12¼.   24187-4 Pa. **$12.95**

COMPLETE CONCERTI GROSSI IN FULL SCORE, Arcangelo Corelli. All 12 concerti in the famous late nineteenth-century edition prepared by violinist Joseph Joachim and musicologist Friedrich Chrysander. 240pp. 8⅜ × 11¼.   25606-5 Pa. **$12.95**

WATER MUSIC AND MUSIC FOR THE ROYAL FIREWORKS IN FULL SCORE, George Frideric Handel. Full scores of two of the most popular Baroque orchestral works performed today—reprinted from definitive Deutsche Handelgesellschaft edition. Total of 96pp. 8¾ × 11.   25070-9 Pa. **$6.95**

LATER SYMPHONIES, Wolfgang A. Mozart. Full orchestral scores to last symphonies (Nos. 35–41) reproduced from definitive Breitkopf & Härtel Complete Works edition. Study score. 285pp. 9 × 12.   23052-X Pa. **$11.95**

17 DIVERTIMENTI FOR VARIOUS INSTRUMENTS, Wolfgang A. Mozart. Sparkling pieces of great vitality and brilliance from 1771–1779; consecutively numbered from 1 to 17. Reproduced from definitive Breitkopf & Härtel Complete Works edition. Study score. 241pp. 9⅜ × 12¼.   23862-8 Pa. **$11.95**

PIANO CONCERTOS NOS. 11–16 IN FULL SCORE, Wolfgang Amadeus Mozart. Authoritative Breitkopf & Härtel edition of six staples of the concerto repertoire, including Mozart's cadenzas for Nos. 12–16. 256pp. 9⅜ × 12¼.   25468-2 Pa. **$12.95**

PIANO CONCERTOS NOS. 17–22, Wolfgang Amadeus Mozart. Six complete piano concertos in full score, with Mozart's own cadenzas for Nos. 17–19. Breitkopf & Härtel edition. Study score. 370pp. 9⅜ × 12¼.   23599-8 Pa. **$14.95**

PIANO CONCERTOS NOS. 23–27, Wolfgang Amadeus Mozart. Mozart's last five piano concertos in full score, plus cadenzas for Nos. 23 and 27, and the Concert Rondo in D Major, K.382. Breitkopf & Härtel edition. Study score. 310pp. 9⅜ × 12¼.   23600-5 Pa. **$12.95**

CONCERTI FOR WIND INSTRUMENTS IN FULL SCORE, Wolfgang Amadeus Mozart. Exceptional volume contains ten pieces for orchestra and wind instruments and includes some of Mozart's finest, most popular music. 272pp. 9⅜ × 12¼.   25228-0 Pa. **$12.95**

THE VIOLIN CONCERTI AND THE SINFONIA CONCERTANTE, K.364, IN FULL SCORE, Wolfgang Amadeus Mozart. All five violin concerti and famed double concerto reproduced from authoritative Breitkopf & Härtel Complete Works Edition. 208pp. 9⅜ × 12½.   25169-1 Pa. **$11.95**

SYMPHONIES 88–92 IN FULL SCORE: The Haydn Society Edition, Joseph Haydn. Full score of symphonies Nos. 88 through 92. Large, readable noteheads, ample margins for fingerings, etc., and extensive Editor's Commentary. 304pp. 9 × 12. (Available in U.S. only)   24445-8 Pa. **$13.95**

COMPLETE LONDON SYMPHONIES IN FULL SCORE, Series I and Series II, Joseph Haydn. Reproduced from the Eulenburg editions are Symphonies Nos. 93–98 (Series I) and Nos. 99–104 (Series II). 800pp. 8⅜ × 11¼. (Available in U.S. only)   Series I 24982-4 Pa. **$15.95**   Series II 24983-2 Pa. **$16.95**

FOUR SYMPHONIES IN FULL SCORE, Franz Schubert. Schubert's four most popular symphonies: No. 4 in C Minor ("Tragic"); No. 5 in B-flat Major; No. 8 in B Minor ("Unfinished"); and No. 9 in C Major ("Great"). Breitkopf & Härtel edition. Study score. 261pp. 9⅜ × 12¼.   23681-1 Pa. **$11.95**

GREAT OVERTURES IN FULL SCORE, Carl Maria von Weber. Overtures to *Oberon, Der Freischutz, Euryanthe* and *Preciosa* reprinted from auhoritative Breitkopf & Härtel editions. 112pp. 9 × 12.   25225-6 Pa. **$8.95**

SYMPHONIES NOS. 1, 2, 3, AND 4 IN FULL SCORE, Ludwig van Beethoven. Republication of H. Litolff edition. 272pp. 9 × 12.   26033-X Pa. **$10.95**

SYMPHONIES NOS. 5, 6 AND 7 IN FULL SCORE, Ludwig van Beethoven. Republication of the H. Litolff edition. 272pp. 9 × 12.   26034-8 Pa. **$10.95**

SYMPHONIES NOS. 8 AND 9 IN FULL SCORE, Ludwig van Beethoven. Republication of the H. Litolff edition. 256pp. 9 × 12.   26035-6 Pa. **$10.95**

SIX GREAT OVERTURES IN FULL SCORE, Ludwig van Beethoven. Six staples of the orchestral repertoire from authoritative Breitkopf & Härtel edition. *Leonore Overtures*, Nos. 1–3; Overtures to *Coriolanus, Egmont, Fidelio.* 288pp. 9 × 12.   24789-9 Pa. **$12.95**

COMPLETE PIANO CONCERTOS IN FULL SCORE, Ludwig van Beethoven. Complete scores of five great Beethoven piano concertos, with all cadenzas as he wrote them, reproduced from authoritative Breitkopf & Härtel edition. New table of contents. 384pp. 9⅜ × 12¼.   24563-2 Pa. **$14.95**

GREAT ROMANTIC VIOLIN CONCERTI IN FULL SCORE, Ludwig van Beethoven, Felix Mendelssohn and Peter Ilyitch Tchaikovsky. The Beethoven Op. 61, Mendelssohn, Op. 64 and Tchaikovsky, Op. 35 concertos reprinted from the Breitkopf & Härtel editions. 224pp. 9 × 12.   24989-1 Pa. **$10.95**

MAJOR ORCHESTRAL WORKS IN FULL SCORE, Felix Mendelssohn. Generally considered to be Mendelssohn's finest orchestral works, here in one volume are: the complete *Midsummer Night's Dream; Hebrides Overture; Calm Sea and Prosperous Voyage Overture;* Symphony No. 3 in A ("Scottish"); and Symphony No. 4 in A ("Italian"). Breitkopf & Härtel edition. Study score. 406pp. 9 × 12.   23184-4 Pa. **$16.95**

COMPLETE SYMPHONIES, Johannes Brahms. Full orchestral scores. No. 1 in C Minor, Op. 68; No. 2 in D Major, Op. 73; No. 3 in F Major, Op. 90; and No. 4 in E Minor, Op. 98. Reproduced from definitive Vienna Gesellschaft der Musikfreunde edition. Study score. 344pp. 9 × 12.   23053-8 Pa. **$13.95**

*Available from your music dealer or write for **free** Music Catalog to Dover Publications, Inc., Dept. MUBI, 31 East 2nd Street, Mineola, N.Y. 11501.*

Dover Orchestral Scores

THREE ORCHESTRAL WORKS IN FULL SCORE: Academic Festival Overture, Tragic Overture and Variations on a Theme by Joseph Haydn, Johannes Brahms. Reproduced from the authoritative Breitkopf & Härtel edition three of Brahms's great orchestral favorites. Editor's commentary in German and English. 112pp. 9⅜ × 12¼.
24637-X Pa. **$8.95**

COMPLETE CONCERTI IN FULL SCORE, Johannes Brahms. Piano Concertos Nos. 1 and 2; Violin Concerto, Op. 77; Concerto for Violin and Cello, Op. 102. Definitive Breitkopf & Härtel edition. 352pp. 9⅜ × 12¼.
24170-X Pa. **$14.95**

COMPLETE SYMPHONIES IN FULL SCORE, Robert Schumann. No. 1 in B-flat Major, Op. 38 ("Spring"); No. 2 in C Major, Op. 61; No. 3 in E Flat Major, Op. 97 ("Rhenish"); and No. 4 in D Minor, Op. 120. Breitkopf & Härtel editions. Study score. 416pp. 9⅜ × 12¼.
24013-4 Pa. **$17.95**

GREAT WORKS FOR PIANO AND ORCHESTRA IN FULL SCORE, Robert Schumann. Collection of three superb pieces for piano and orchestra, including the popular Piano Concerto in A Minor. Breitkopf & Härtel edition. 183pp. 9⅜ × 12¼.
24340-0 Pa. **$9.95**

THE PIANO CONCERTOS IN FULL SCORE, Frédéric Chopin. The authoritative Breitkopf & Härtel full-score edition in one volume of Piano Concertos No. 1 in E Minor and No. 2 in F Minor. 176pp. 9 × 12.
25835-1 Pa. **$9.95**

THE PIANO CONCERTI IN FULL SCORE, Franz Liszt. Available in one volume the Piano Concerto No. 1 in E-flat Major and the Piano Concerto No. 2 in A Major—are among the most studied, recorded and performed of all works for piano and orchestra. 144pp. 9 × 12.
25221-3 Pa. **$8.95**

SYMPHONY NO. 8 IN G MAJOR, OP. 88, SYMPHONY NO. 9 IN E MINOR, OP. 95 ("NEW WORLD") IN FULL SCORE, Antonín Dvořák. Two celebrated symphonies by the great Czech composer, the Eighth and the immensely popular Ninth, "From the New World" in one volume. 272pp. 9 × 12.
24749-X Pa. **$12.95**

FOUR ORCHESTRAL WORKS IN FULL SCORE: Rapsodie Espagnole, Mother Goose Suite, Valses Nobles et Sentimentales, and Pavane for a Dead Princess, Maurice Ravel. Four of Ravel's most popular orchestral works, reprinted from original full-score French editions. 240pp. 9⅜ × 12¼. (Not available in France or Germany)
25962-5 Pa. **$11.95**

DAPHNIS AND CHLOE IN FULL SCORE, Maurice Ravel. Definitive full-score edition of Ravel's rich musical setting of a Greek fable by Longus is reprinted here from the original French edition. 320pp. 9⅜ × 12¼. (Not available in France or Germany)
25826-2 Pa. **$14.95**

THREE GREAT ORCHESTRAL WORKS IN FULL SCORE, Claude Debussy. Three favorites by influential modernist: *Prélude à l'Après-midi d'un Faune*, *Nocturnes*, and *La Mer*. Reprinted from early French editions. 279pp. 9 × 12.
24441-5 Pa. **$12.95**

SYMPHONY IN D MINOR IN FULL SCORE, César Franck. Superb, authoritative edition of Franck's only symphony, an often-performed and recorded masterwork of late French romantic style. 160pp. 9 × 12.
25373-2 Pa. **$9.95**

THE GREAT WALTZES IN FULL SCORE, Johann Strauss, Jr. Complete scores of eight melodic masterpieces: The Beautiful Blue Danube, Emperor Waltz, Tales of the Vienna Woods, Wiener Blut, four more. Authoritative editions. 336pp. 8⅜ × 11¼.
26009-7 Pa. **$13.95**

FOURTH, FIFTH AND SIXTH SYMPHONIES IN FULL SCORE, Peter Ilyitch Tchaikovsky. Complete orchestral scores of Symphony No. 4 in F minor, Op. 36; Symphony No. 5 in E minor, Op. 64; Symphony No. 6 in B minor, "Pathetique," Op. 74. Study score. Breitkopf & Härtel editions. 480pp. 9⅜ × 12¼.
23861-X Pa. **$19.95**

ROMEO AND JULIET OVERTURE AND CAPRICCIO ITALIEN IN FULL SCORE, Peter Ilyitch Tchaikovsky. Two of Russian master's most popular compositions in high quality, inexpensive reproduction. From authoritative Russian edition. 208pp. 8⅜ × 11½.
25217-5 Pa. **$9.95**

NUTCRACKER SUITE IN FULL SCORE, Peter Ilyitch Tchaikovsky. Among the most popular ballet pieces ever created—a complete, inexpensive, high-quality score to study and enjoy. 128pp. 9 × 12.
25379-1 Pa. **$7.95**

TONE POEMS, SERIES I: DON JUAN, TOD UND VERKLA-RUNG, and DON QUIXOTE, Richard Strauss. Three of the most often performed and recorded works in entire orchestral repertoire, reproduced in full score from original editions. Study score. 286pp. 9⅜ × 12¼. (Available in U.S. only)
23754-0 Pa. **$13.95**

TONE POEMS, SERIES II: TILL EULENSPIEGELS LUSTIGE STREICHE, ALSO SPRACH ZARATHUSTRA, and EIN HEL-DENLEBEN, Richard Strauss. Three important orchestral works, including very popular *Till Eulenspiegel's Merry Pranks*, reproduced in full score from original editions. Study score. 315pp. 9⅜ × 12¼. (Available in U.S. only)
23755-9 Pa. **$14.95**

DAS LIED VON DER ERDE IN FULL SCORE, Gustav Mahler. Mahler's masterpiece, a fusion of song and symphony, reprinted from the original 1912 Universal Edition. English translations of song texts. 160pp. 9 × 12.
25657-X Pa. **$8.95**

SYMPHONIES NOS. 1 AND 2 IN FULL SCORE, Gustav Mahler. Unabridged, authoritative Austrian editions of Symphony No. 1 in D Major ("Titan") and Symphony No. 2 in C Minor ("Resurrection"). 384pp. 8⅛ × 11.
25473-9 Pa. **$14.95**

SYMPHONIES NOS. 3 AND 4 IN FULL SCORE, Gustav Mahler. Two brilliantly contrasting masterworks—one scored for a massive ensemble, the other for small orchestra and soloist—reprinted from authoritative Viennese editions. 368pp. 9⅜ × 12¼.
26166-2 Pa. **$15.95**

SYMPHONY NO. 8 IN FULL SCORE, Gustav Mahler. Superb authoritative edition of massive, complex "Symphony of a Thousand." Scored for orchestra, eight solo voices, double chorus, boys' choir and organ. Reprint of Izdatel'stvo "Muzyka," Moscow, edition. Translation of texts. 272pp. 9⅜ × 12¼.
26022-4 Pa. **$12.95**

THE FIREBIRD IN FULL SCORE (Original 1910 Version), Igor Stravinsky. Handsome, inexpensive edition of modern masterpiece, renowned for brilliant orchestration, glowing color. Authoritative Russian edition. 176pp. 9⅜ × 12¼. (Available in U.S. only)
25535-2 Pa. **$9.95**

PETRUSHKA IN FULL SCORE: Original Version, Igor Stravinsky. The definitive full-score edition of Stravinsky's masterful score for the great Ballets Russes 1911 production of *Petrushka*. 160pp. 9⅜ × 12¼. (Available in U.S. only)
25680-4 Pa. **$9.95**

THE RITE OF SPRING IN FULL SCORE, Igor Stravinsky. A reprint of the original full-score edition of the most famous musical work of the 20th century, created as a ballet score for Diaghilev's Ballets Russes. 176pp. 9⅜ × 12¼. (Available in U.S. only)
25857-2 Pa. **$9.95**

Available from your music dealer or write for free Music Catalog to Dover Publications, Inc., Dept. MUBI, 31 East 2nd Street, Mineola, N.Y. 11501.